Take Time to Stop Smoking

A How Not to Smoke Handbook

RICHARD LYNN SHEPHERD

EDITED BY JASON REEVES

This book belongs to:

Legal Jazz

Copyright © 2018, 2019 Take Time to Stop Smoking
by Richard Lynn Shepherd
All rights reserved. No part of this book may be used or reproduced in any manner without written permission from the author, except in the case of brief quotations embodied in articles and reviews.

ISBN-13: 978-1722927059
ISBN-10: 1722927054

Book layout provided by
SelfPublishMe.com - Publishing consulting and book design services for independent authors.

Acknowledgments

Desaray C.
Ronnie Calloway
Darryl & Christa @ Sherman-Hume Insurance
John Ferguson
L.D. Ferguson
Tony Garcia
Gary Garrison and Chad Ricker
The Gavula Brothers, Joe and George
Dave Gray
Roy Greene – Friends For Fifty Years!
Luther Hodges
Don and Ann Holbrook
Denise Hart
Danny Hobbs
Judylynn
Bob and Karen Ketts
Scott Lock
Joseph Maly
Patrick Mannix
Debbie Mahan, RN
Micaela
William Henry McKenney
Beth Minster
DeLila Noland
Steve Sanders
Michelle Schroeder
Robert D. Shepherd
... and last, but certainly not least, THE "Z" MAN!

Families
The Skye Doggett Family
The Ervin Family
The Scott Finley Family
Teresa Hibbs, her Wife and Family
Stephen Owens Family

The Tasha Stewart Family
The Charmane Thrower Family

The Doctors
Dr. Thomas Joyce
Rev. Dr. Doug and Cheryl Samples
Steve B. Skarky MD

The Music Makers
Richard Blankenship and Emma Lee
Kyle Dillingham and Horseshoe Road (with Peter Markes and Brent Saulsbury)
Jim Hoke
Maurice Johnson
Tom Lienke

The Virtual Daughters
Chelsey
Andrea Parker
Paige Short
Sarah Tabor

The Librarians
Metro Library, Bethany, Ok
The Three Graces – Edie Daniel, Debbie McPherson, and Janet Bowen
Metro Library, Downtown, OKC
Samuel Karnes
Metro Library, Edmond, Ok
Ms. Adrien Fisher
Ms. Darcus Smith
Metro Library, Warr Acres, Ok
Donna Durbin

Table of Contents

Dedication

My Mission

Forward

Time   12

Warning   14

Fire!   17

Health   19

Hard Things to Do   22

The Child   24

Sharon   26

Judylynn   28

Anger   30

Pride   32

Love   34

Fear   36

Money   38

Society   40

Mind - Body - Spirit   44

You   46

On the Day of My Birth   49

My Smoking Years. This is How
I Made Them History! 51

Experiment 55

Dad 57

Mom 63

The Future 68

Dedication

This book is dedicated to you, the smoker, who has the courage to take that first step onto the path that will lead to the day you become smoke free. I wish you good health and every happiness.
—RICHARD LYNN SHEPHERD

"A journey of a thousand miles must begin with a single step."
—LAOZI, Chinese philosopher and writer. Born 601 BC

"Difficult roads often lead to beautiful destinations."
—ZIG ZIGLAR, American author and motivational speaker 1926-2012

My Mission

This is a very simple book built around a very simple idea. Herein, I only have words and a few stories, quotes, and illustrations to convince you to dedicate yourself to quitting smoking for the rest of your life. Do this for yourself, for those whom you love and love you, and for a longer, healthier life and all that you hold dear.
    -RLS

Forward

Years ago I was having blood drawn at my doctor's office for cholesterol and thyroid tests. The new nurse, whom I had never met, said she had looked at my chart and noticed I hadn't had a PSA test. (PSA testing is a way to catch prostate cancer, hopefully before it spreads to other areas.) At that time, they usually would recommend the PSA test around age 50. I said "Well, I'm only 48, but as long as you are drawing blood, help yourself to a little more".

When the test results came back, I was told my PSA score was kind of high. So, I made an appointment with the urologist that had performed surgery on me 3 years before. The next step was to biopsy my prostate. I had cancer, but in a very early stage. My urologist convinced me to allow him to remove my prostate.

The PSA test can be a real lifesaver. Before the PSA, by the time a man knew something was wrong, it was often too late.

So there went my prostate and the cancer with it. I now know that I should have gone to the urologist that my doctor recommended, but let me just say, always get a second opinion.

I made up my mind that I was going to save a man's life, so I started polling male customers where I was working and asking them if they had ever heard of the PSA test. Most hadn't, and I told them it was a simple blood test and they should do it.

About a year later, a man named Bill came in and asked if I recognized him. I told him I remembered his face. He said I had told him about PSA testing a year before and they had found cancer. I asked him how he was doing and he said he would know in a month or so and would come back to see me.

A month later he came in and said he was cancer free, and that I had saved his life! I told him I couldn't thank him enough. He was surprised at this and asked why I was thanking him. I told him it was a two way street and it had been my intent to save a man's life. You see, every now and then I feel that I've grown into the man my father wanted me to be.

When I saw Bill again, we had a chance to sit down and talk. He told me that he had been at stage four cancer and they had pulled him back all the way! He had taken an early retirement, bought an acreage, put a trailer on it, met a woman, got married and they were building a house. He has more life.

Sometime later, I was telling another man this story, and he leaned in close and said. "You never know whose life you might save if you take time to save your own".

Please, let me help you save yours.

TIME

The title of this book is: "Take time to stop smoking"

Our lives are made of and measured by time. We just don't know how much we are to be given. It's a surprise package, and we can't buy more. We can only try to take good care of ourselves so we have the time to do what needs to be done.

I heard this quote years ago.

"Give me work until the end of my time and time until the end of my work".

If you use my method, it will require an investment of time. Remember, it's your time, so use it to your best advantage. As a smoker, you have one of the most important decisions that you will ever make in your life. Deciding to quit smoking for the rest of the days you are gifted.

There is an important difference between stopping and quitting. When you stop, you are taking a break from smoking. You are fasting. When you quit, that's it! You are a nonsmoker, never to go back to it. How do you know when you have quit? Trust yourself, you'll know. It's when you have stopped, a measure of time has gone by, and it becomes apparent that you are ready to leave your habit behind.

I can't offer a guarantee that my method will work for you. That depends entirely on you. However, if you use this method and stop often, you will be saving money when you aren't smoking and the book will pay for itself.

Now, Let's Begin...

"What you can do or dream you can, begin it; Boldness has genius, power, and magic in it." - Irish Poet John Anster, Inspired by Johann Wolfgang Von Goethe's *"Faust"*

Do you have a smoker's cough? You may have had it so long that you no longer notice it, or don't relate it to smoking. A pulmonary specialist may likely diagnose it as bronchitis, which is the inflammation of the mucous membrane in the bronchial tubes. It typically causes bronchospasm and coughing. This is an early warning sign that you absolutely must quit smoking or face permanent, irreversible damage to your lungs.

Emphysema – A condition in which the air sacs of the lungs are damaged and enlarged, causing breathlessness.

C.O.P.D. – Chronic obstructive pulmonary disease is a lung disease characterized by chronic obstruction of lung airflow that interferes with normal breathing and is not fully reversible. The more familiar terms, "chronic bronchitis" and "emphysema" are no longer used, but are now included within the C.O.P.D. diagnosis.

Throat Cancer – A group of cancers of the mouth, sinuses, nose, or throat. A cough and voice changes are common symptoms of throat cancer.

Lung Cancer – the uncontrolled growth of abnormal cells that start off in one or both lungs, usually in the cells that line the air passages.

The abnormal cells do not develop into healthy lung tissue. They divide rapidly and form tumors.

Cancer Metastasized – In metastasis, cancer cells break away from where they first formed (primary cancer) travel through the blood or lymph system, and form new tumors in other parts of the body.

The above isn't even close to the end of the list. There are many more harmful effects from a long term smoking addiction.

These are the basic facts. These are the risks that smokers must face.

In my humble opinion on the half shell...

SMOKING IS POISONOUS!

You don't have to take my word for it. Go to the library and/or get on the internet and read the long list of the areas of the body that are affected by smoking and the known dangerous and toxic compounds that go into manufacturing tobacco products. I trust that you'll agree.

"A cigarette is the only consumer product which used as directed kills the consumer."

-GRO HARLEM BRUNDTLAND, Former prime minister of Norway

FIRE!
THAT'S RIGHT, YOU ARE PLAYING WITH FIRE!

Poetry Break!

I met a man named Mr. Brown

He told me that his house burned down

All the way to the ground

I did indeed meet a man named Mr. Brown and his house did burn down to the ground. Gratefully, no one was home. His daughter was visiting a neighbor. It happened within the first couple of weeks of December, almost Christmas.

You may think you know where I'm going with this, but no, I'm not. In this case, the fire started from an electrical short and not from someone smoking. All that was left was the fireplace and chimney, so he's rebuilding. He said it was going to be a log cabin style home, and was planning on turning the hearth and chimney into an outdoor patio fireplace. Isn't that cool and classy?

We had a pleasant conversation. The reason for this little story? He said to me, "I'm just looking to do the next right thing." Remember this, please. You may stop and realize how just one right decision can make a world of difference in your life. Just one!

If you are truly serious about getting the smoking habit behind you, make it the next right thing you do.

"It is common knowledge that smoking is considered one of the nation's leading causes of preventable death, but it's less widely known that cigarettes are also the leading cause of fatal fires."

–ED MARLEY, Democratic U.S. Senator from Massachusetts

HEALTH

Nurse Debbie Says:
"Don't you want to feel better?"

"The greatest of follies is to sacrifice health for any other kind of happiness."

–ARTHUR SCHOPENHAUER, German Philosopher
1788 - 1860

As a smoker, quitting is the single most effective action you can take to greatly improve your overall health, but please, don't stop there! You should try to see the larger picture and include improvements in exercise, nutrition, sleep, loving, stress reduction, etc. If you're going to take the big step to get tobacco out of your life, move ahead by improving every aspect of healthy living.

"I have decided to be happy, because it's good for my health." – VOLTAIRE 1694 – 1778, French enlightenment writer, historian, and philosopher famous for his wit.

There are many over the counter products that can help you quit. Nicotine gum, patches, lozenges, as well as doctor prescribed pharmaceuticals. Some people even try hypnosis.

If you really feel the need to have something to help, I would like to guide you to a health food store or natural pharmacy. They have herbs, organics, and lots of good advice that can help you with some of the negative effects of breaking the smoking addiction.

Another suggestion is to go to a steam room or sauna. I believe it will help you sweat out toxins and could make it easier to quit.

We really can't overestimate how much exercise will help when you stop or quit smoking. I love to walk! Getting out and getting fresh air into your lungs instead of smoke is another thing you can do. Our lungs were not designed to breathe smoke. You should keep in mind that air pollution, especially in cities, is an ever growing concern. Not smoking and keeping your lungs healthy will help protect you from what's in the air that we have little or no control over.

"Health isn't everything, but without health, everything else is nothing."

–Arthur Schopenhauer

Remember !

"Your body will start repairing itself immediately after you smoke your last cigarette !"
RLS

HARD THINGS TO DO

Quitting smoking is hard, but well worth it! It is hard to say yes to quitting, and easy to say no. Consider that the people who have the most power and authority are not the ones that can say "no". They are the ones who say "yes".

I worked in a book store for over a decade as the main cashier. I saw everything that came over the counter, and reading titles all day is an education in and of itself. One of the books I remember is, "Do Hard Things – A teen rebellion against low expectations", and was written by twin brothers Alex and Brett Harris. (Published by Waterbrook Multnomah, a division of Random House, April 15, 2008). The book encourages teenagers to go beyond their comfort zone and challenge themselves to reach beyond their grasp by doing hard things.

There is a life lesson here. As adults, we are often looking to find the easiest way, the shortcuts, and the quickest way from point A to point B. In doing so, we lose sight of how taking on the hard things will help up grow and develop. So, here's your challenge:

Recognize that quitting smoking is hard, but take it on, work through it, and make it happen. Don't make it harder than it needs to be. You can do this!

"We choose to go to the moon in this decade and do the other things, not because they are easy, but because they are hard."

–JOHN F. KENNEDY 1917 – 1963

35TH President of the United States of America

THE CHILD

"Out of the mouth of babes..." Psalms 8.2

Years ago I was visiting my friend, Jay Ervin, at a big house he shared with roommates. After a while we decided to go get some supper. While everyone got ready to go, I went out the door and down to the sidewalk to smoke.

Suddenly, I noticed there was a child watching me. I guessed this little person to be about 8 years old, but around that age and how they were dressed, I wasn't certain if I was looking at a boy or girl.

The child seemed to have just suddenly appeared, and with a sad, sad face said, "That's not good for you". I was stunned! I had often felt ashamed and embarrassed about children seeing me smoke. This was the first time a child had said anything to me about it, and with a truly honest concern for my health. I took it to heart, and I'll always remember it.

...And a little child will lead them." Isaiah 11:6.

SHARON

Back in the early 70's, my brother had a lady friend named Sharon who came to visit us here in Oklahoma City. She was from Pierce City, Mo, which is 5 miles from Monett, our home town. That was the first time she and I met.

She was an earthy, hippy woman and was just loaded with love and goodness. She had lots of knowledge about natural foods, remedies, and healthy living.

She came to town to see us two or three times. When she would see me smoking, she would say, "Oh, that's so bad for you! It's a terrible plant. You really should quit." My reply was, "Oh, I know I should, but it's so hard to quit." Then she said something that surprised me. "Just blow it off!" "What?" Then she said it again. Could it really be that easy? So, I tried it. When I got the urge to smoke, I would just shrug it off with one shoulder and turn my attention to something else. I didn't smoke again for seven months.

One day, I walked into a favorite hangout and saw a friend who didn't smoke… smoking. He had some imported cigarettes, and offered me one. That's all it took. Just one. I thought I could smoke one "now and then", but I was wrong. Before long I was back to smoking a pack a day.

A few years later, a Doctor told me to quit smoking. He said I had bronchitis. I didn't know how long it would take, but I had done it before and I knew I could stop again. I just knew it!

As you use my stopping method, see how long you can go without smoking. Just blow it off!

"You have not failed until you quit trying."

-Gordon B. Hinckley 1910 – 2008, American religious leader

Remember !

The urge to smoke will pass whether you smoke or not.

JUDYLYNN

Judylynn is a gal pal of mine. I think she's fearless. She doesn't think so, but it sure seems to me she's living a life without fear. Maybe it's because she's from New York.

We've been close friends for a few decades now, but hey, who's counting? All I know is, we haven't been friends long enough.

Like myself, Judylynn was a smoker for many years. She stopped smoking cigarettes when her first grandchild was born and took up vaping. Now, I'll allow that vaping is perhaps somewhat safer than cigarettes, but by how much? As yet, "they" haven't figured that out. It seems to me that vaping is just exchanging one bad habit for another. For Judylynn, it was just a stepping stone. After some time went by, this great lady quit vaping, joined a gym, adjusted her diet, and made other healthy and positive life choices.

Now, she is smoke free and she says she doesn't miss it at all. Not at all.

ANGER

Smoking creates anger. The smokers are angry because they find themselves unwelcome in more places than ever before. These days, smoking is not allowed or is illegal in nearly every building, public and private. Are you having to stand out in the heat, rain, or freezing cold to smoke? To those who see people outside in all kinds of weather smoking, it only underscores what a sad lot smokers really are. Many smokers will defend their smoking habit all the way to the cemetery!

Nonsmokers are angry because they are forced to breathe second hand smoke, which has been discovered to be harmful.

Now, here's what makes me angry! People who smoke around babies, children, and pets. They aren't taking away someone's choice not to breathe smoke. They are exposing those who have no choice!

My brother was dating a woman when her twin sister came to town for a visit. She was a smoker. I was telling her about my plans to write this book and she got angry at me and said, "Well, there's nothing worse than a reformed smoker!" My reply was, "Maybe to a smoker, but many nonsmokers think there is nothing better." To this she said...nothing.

"If you are an angry smoker, get angry enough to quit." –RLS

PRIDE

"Quitting smoking can be a very good test of one's character. Pass the test and you will have accomplished so much more than just get rid of one bad habit."

–Abraham Maslow, American Psychologist

1908 – 1970.

He is known for Maslow's Hierarchy of Needs.

(You would do well for yourself to look this up.)

So it is, and so it can be for you. It was something that happened to me after I became a nonsmoker. I proved to myself that I could do something difficult that would make my life better, and have a positive effect on others. It also gave me the courage to want to take on other difficult tasks.

"I'm more proud of quitting smoking than anything else I've done in my life, including winning an Oscar." CHRISTINE LAHTI –Actress and Filmmaker

I wish to advise you to be wise!

Now, don't try to impress anyone with how smart you are and then light a cigarette. Likely, they aren't going to think you are smart at all. However, if you tell others that you were a smoker, and you haven't smoked in days, (or weeks, or months, or years,) they will look at you very differently.

Work to dispel shame and guilt and replace it with pride. Like fear, shame and guilt do not serve you and will make it all the more difficult to stop and eventually quit smoking.

Now, just think of the things that you have said and done in your life that you are most proud of. Quitting smoking and getting it further and further behind you will say something important about you to others, and to yourself.

"Take pride in how far you've come. Have faith in how far you can go, but don't forget to enjoy the journey" –MICHAEL JOSEPHSON - Speaker and former law professor

A How Not to Smoke Handbook

LOVE

LOVE! Is there anything better in this life? I love life, love this world, and I never run out of people to love!

"THOU SHALT LOVE THY NEIGHBOR AS THYSELF"
MATTHEW 22:31

Do you think the reverse could also be true? To love yourself as you would your neighbor?
I believe you can't truly love others without loving yourself. I think it's basic to survival and a happy life.

"You, yourself, just as much as anyone in the entire universe, deserve your love and affection." –BUDDA

I'm writing this book with love for you. Count on it. Most people can't imagine having love for people they don't know and will likely never meet. It's true though, and without it I don't think

I would have ever learned to love and respect myself.

Many years ago, when I was still a smoker, I was dating a woman who didn't smoke. Perhaps she never did. She once said, "I don't like your smoking because it takes you away from me."
I remember it because it was surely true. Smokers put friends and loved ones ON HOLD while they run off somewhere to smoke.

Something you may come to realize after you have stopped smoking for a while, or have quit for good:

SMOKING STINKS!

Most smokers don't realize how bad they smell. It gets in your hair, your skin, your clothes, your furniture, your car, and everything else. If you are a smoker and trying to attract someone to love, you may have to settle for a smoker and codependence.

So quitting smoking is an act of love for yourself, love for others, and for those who love you.

FEAR

FALSE EVIDENCE APPEARING REAL

"The enemy is fear. We think it is hate; but it is fear." –GANDHI 1869 – 1948

In the book, "A Course in Miracles", it says that there are two primary emotions, love and fear. All the positive emotions come from love and all the negative emotions from fear. I've found this to be food for thought. If you watch how someone behaves and listen to what they are saying, it's often easy to determine if their life is generally propelled by love or fear.

I choose love over fear, and I believe you should too. If you are fearful of quitting smoking and give in to that fear, it can and will add more time to your habit. Maybe even years. Be thee not afraid! Choose love. Quitting smoking is an act of love and should be a guiding choice to become a nonsmoker.

"The only thing we have to fear is fe

–FRANKLIN D. ROOSEVELT, 1828 - 19⁴

32ND President of the United States America

"You gain strength, courage, and confidence by every experience in which you really stop to look fear in the face. You must do the thing which you think you cannot do."

–ELEANOR ROOSEVELT, 1884 - 1962

Franklin D. Roosevelt's First Lady

The smoking addiction is just
another form of
PRISON !

MONEY

Let's talk about money. How much do you spend on a pack of cigarettes? How much for a carton? When I first started smoking, cigarettes were 30 or 35 cents a pack. These days you can expect to pay $6 to $8 a pack and over $50 a carton.

Something I've started doing is adding up how much I spend on anything I use regularly to get an idea of the cost for a full year. Say you buy them by the pack and smoke a pack a day. That's over $2000 a year! Now, what would you do with an extra $2000 once you quit smoking?

I've created a list to help you get started:

Donations, family vacation, furniture, new clothes, a better car, gifts for the family and friends, pay bills, pay off loans, take a college course, etc.

You get the idea. Use your imagination and write your list in the journal at the back of this book.

You may want to put what you would be spending on tobacco into a savings account.
I sure wish I had done this when I quit smoking over thirty years ago. It's your money so you decide, but I recommend you invest in life instead of illness and death.

Poetry Break!

ALLITERATION

The occurrence of the same letter or sound at the beginning of adjacent or closely connected words.

Example: *"People profiting by placing a problem in your pocket".* -RLS

SOCIETY

"The true face of smoking is disease, death and horror – not the glamour and sophistication the pushers in the tobacco industry try to portray."

–DAVID BYRNE, American musician known for his group, Talking Heads

My parents smoked and, of course, I naturally wanted to be like my parents. When I was growing up in the 50's and 60's, I believe the majority of adults were smokers. It was accepted as normal. Cigarette advertising was on radio and television, print advertising in newspapers and magazines, on billboards coast to coast, and nearly every actor smoked in movies and TV productions. Cigarette vending machines were everywhere. There was seldom anyone around to stop the underaged from putting money in an unguarded vending machine. I started early and smoking became part of my self image. I was cool, or I thought I was. Society said it was alright to do because it was part of life.

These days it is just the reverse. Each state in the union has a minimum age (from 18 to 21) to buy tobacco products and identification is required as proof. I can't remember the last time I saw a cigarette vending machine.

These days, tobacco advertising is limited. There are antismoking messages, and all kinds of help with smoking cessation, and still people smoke. Why do some of us smoke, drink alcohol, and take consciousness altering substances? One reason is, because we have the free time to do so.

The tobacco smoking habit has been with us for centuries. My grandparents generation and generations that came before were not the kind of smokers we have today. A cigarette in the mouth, one in the hand, and another one burning up in the ashtray. In the past, most people had to work as hard as they could from almost sunup to after dark just to earn enough money to provide food, clothing, and shelter for their families. They didn't have time to smoke all day. They may have smoked a little with their noonday meal, smoked some by the fire in the evening, and then off to bed to get rest so they could work hard the next day.

Take a moment to stop and think about your ancestors. Your parents, grandparents, great grandparents, and all of the greats that came before them. You are living proof that everything they did and all they went through was so you could be right here, right now! Please honor them by taking great care of yourself, and honor them by quitting smoking.

"Parents should not smoke in order to discourage their kids from smoking. A child is more likely to smoke when they have been raised in the environment of a smoker."

–Christy Turlington, American model, charity-founder and campaigner, and filmmaker.

While writing this book, I didn't intend it to be an attack on the tobacco industry. This book was created to help you quit smoking. However, I do have an example of how they think. As I understand it, when you smoke imported cigarettes from some foreign countries, many of them only burn while you are smoking them. You put it down and they go out. American cigarettes are designed and manufactured to continue to burn if you lay it down somewhere. It seems they don't care if you smoke it or not. All they want is for you to buy them and fire them up. As long as it's burning, they make money. Sounds like a fire hazard to me.

"These are the days that people who quit smoking are celebrated and held up as a good example for others." –RLS

MIND – BODY– SPIRIT

"The greatest discovery of my generation is that a human being can alter his life by altering his attitudes of mind." –WILLIAM JAMES, 1842 - 1910 American Philosopher and Psychologist

Tobacco smoking is an addiction. Calling it a habit is just a nice way to say it. It's a physical and a psychological addiction. First, you should start with the psychological. Make the one decision you must make if you really want to quit. Do I truly want to be a nonsmoker? If the decision is yes, then your choice is made and you set it in stone.

"You are the master, the mind is your servant. That is the correct relationship."

–Sri MOOJI, Spiritual Teacher

Now that you are in command, use your mind to attack the physical addiction. Mind over body. When you feel the urge to smoke, know that it's the physical addiction trying to take over. Since your mind is made up to quit smoking, use your mind to overrule the physical.

Do you believe in a higher power? Do you choose to believe in guardian angels, and consider that loved ones who have passed on watch over you? Then you may wish to ask for Divine Guidance to give you strength to break your addiction. A little faith can go a long way.

"Take the first step in faith. You don't have to see the whole staircase. Just take the first step."

–REV. DR. MARTIN LUTHER KING, 1929 - 1968

YOU!

Quotes for You, and Perhaps About You.

"You are the first person you need to depend on."
–Maurice Johnson, An American Jazz Artist

"You can't start a new chapter of your life if you keep re-reading the last one."
–Anonymous

"You know all those things that you've always wanted to do? You should go do them."
–E. J. Lamprey, Author

"You can't change what's going on around you until you start changing what's going on within you."
–Zig Ziglar

"In some way you should celebrate each day that you do not smoke"
-RLS

"You have to find what sparks a light in you so that you in your own way can illuminate the world."
–OPRAH WINFREY

"You were born with potential. You were born with goodness and trust. You were born with ideals and dreams. You were born with greatness. You were born with wings. You are not meant for crawling, so don't. You have wings. Learn to use them and fly."

–RUMI, 1207 - 1273 13TH Century Persian Sunni Muslim Poet

"You are forgiven for your happiness and your successes only if you generously consent to share them"
–ALBERT CAMUS, 1913 - 1960 French Philosopher, Author, and Journalist

"You can find a better you inside you. Why don't you search for that?"
–MUNIA KHAN, Poet

"In this world there is only one task that only you can do. Only you can keep your word."
–VINEET RAJ KAPOOR, Actor, Producer, and Director

"Hey friend, don't you dare forget, as you're creating a new you, that there's a whole lot about the old you that is worth keeping."
–TONI SORENSON, Mormon Author

"To become a better you, look nowhere else for greatness. All you need to improve and succeed are right there in you."
–ISRAELMORE AYIVOR, Author of
'The Great Handbook of Quotes'

"You can't help who you are, but you can change who you want to be."
–BENNY BELLAMACINA, *Author, Poet, and Songwriter*

"You die in time to realize some things aren't worthwhile."

–DOMINIC RICCITELLO, American internet Personality and Blogger

ON THE DAY OF MY BIRTH

I was born on May 11, 1953. Three things come to mind that I wish I could change. I was induced labor, I was a bottle baby instead of being nursed, and my mother smoked cigarettes for the entire nine months she was pregnant. This was 1953. They didn't know all the dangers of smoking 66 years ago that they now know. So, I was a sick infant. I had trouble keeping formula down, and the hospital staff wasn't being entirely honest with my parents about it. After leaving the hospital, my parents took me to a doctor. As the story goes, the doctor put his fingers out, I grabbed them, and he lifted me right up off the table. My parents were proud I was so strong. The Doctor said, "This isn't good. Richard is very nervous." He didn't know why.

What I now believe is this. I was born addicted to nicotine and was going through withdrawal, starting at birth. The doctor took me off formula and put me on whole milk. It worked.

I often wonder if this is the reason that, once I started smoking, I had such a difficult time quitting. Regardless, I quit!

MY SMOKING YEARS
This is How I Made Them History!

I smoked for 17 years and I quit over 30 years ago. If I hadn't quit for health reasons, surely by now I would have quit out of embarrassment. You may never think of it, but I'm reasonably certain you didn't become a smoker the very first time you tried it.

At a very young age, my best friend and I were acting like we were smokers. We were just lighting them up, drawing in smoke and blowing it out, but we didn't inhale smoke into our lungs. We didn't know it at the time, but when you start inhaling cigarette smoke, that's when you get addicted to nicotine. So, if you didn't become a smoker with your very first cigarette, why would you feel the need to stop cold turkey? Oh, you can, and people do, but you don't have to unless you decide that it's the best way for you.

My method is simple. Set a date and time as close or far away as you wish but, the closer the better. Do remember, this method isn't intended to enable you to stay a smoker, but help you to quit smoking for good and all. So, avoid setting your stop date and time too far in the future!

The stop date/time is also set in stone, like your decision to quit.

When that time arrives,... Stop! You are now fasting. Go as long as you can, or as long as you care to, but don't start smoking again until you have another stop date/ time set. See how long you can go without breaking your fast. Why not? You can have one anytime you want so long as you have another stop date marked in your journal and on your calendar. You may find that as you progress, your fasting will get longer and your smoking period will get shorter. Each time you break your fast and with each cigarette you light up, please think about that day in your future that you smoke your very last cigarette. Think about a better life and look forward to that day!

After several times stopping and starting, you may also find that it's easier to stop and harder to start again. Using this method will show you the difference between how you feel when you smoke and when you don't. Most people don't quit long enough to experience this. In short, you are rehearsing to become a nonsmoker.

This method didn't come to me in a flash. It just evolved. I made a solid decision that I would keep stopping over and over and look forward to the day when I would crush out my last cigarette and never look back. That day arrived!

Something you should not do is tell your family and all your friends that you are quitting. They are likely to form a line, take a number, take a seat, and wait their turn to give you a hard time if they see you smoking. Can't you just hear it? "I thought you quit smoking..." You don't need that brand of negative noise! Just tell one or two people who you can depend on to be supportive.

I do encourage you to use the journal in the back of the book to make notes of dates and times and your thoughts and feelings throughout the process. Review your notes often to track your progress.

This method will only be effective if you are serious about making it work. Please share this book with someone you know who needs to quit smoking.

"There are a multitude of reasons to quit smoking, and not one truly good reason to continue." –RLS

EXPERIMENT

Designing Your Own Program for Quitting Smoking.

You are in control of the entire process of becoming a nonsmoker and getting tobacco out of your life forever. You are in charge. You are the one who can make it happen. These days, there is a great good deal of help from many sources. If this book doesn't provide enough help to guide you, more help is out there and on the way.

Oklahoma Tobacco Helpline. It's free and 24/7

1-800-**quitnow** (1-800-784-8669) OKhelpline.com

If you live in another state, it's likely your state has one too.

American Lung Association – www.lung.org

National Cancer Institute – smokefree.gov

American Cancer Society – www.cancer.org

...and the list goes on and on from here. Go to the library and/or the internet. You never know what you may find that, in some way, will help you with your journey.

DAD

My father, Raymond Dale Shepherd, was born August 4, 1912 to Edward and Anna Shepherd. He came into our world in the family home, 510 W. Logan, in Monett, Missouri. In those days that area of town was known as Chigger Hill. As I remember it, I was told by my Aunt Sib that he went by Ray or Raymond when he was young, but at some point decided to be known as Dale.

This is his story of the sentinel event that injured and scarred our entire family.

Dad served in the Army Air Corp during World War II. He was a master machinist, airplane mechanic, and held the rank of Sergeant. He didn't serve overseas. He was ordered to remain state side and moved around the country working on aircraft to keep them flying.

The war had finally come to an end, and the men and women who survived were coming home to look for jobs and start families. There was still a lot of work to do, so he stayed in the service.

I believe my father was about as fearless as men come. He was a lot like John Wayne. Before he went into the service, he worked at Curtiss – Wright in St. Louis, Mo. People used to stop him on the street and ask him if he WAS John Wayne. At that point in their lives, they did resemble each other quite a bit.

On some unknown date my Dad got aboard a North American B-25J Mitchell for a test flight, performing the duties of flight engineer. The man scheduled to pilot was Col. Robert R. Smith and as it turns out, this was the first time he had ever flown a B-25. The way Colonel Smith piloted this flight frightened my Father so much, that he had Smith written up. Having done that, he was never again supposed to be scheduled to fly with this officer in the cockpit. Think of it! A Sergeant reporting a Colonel as being an unsafe flyer! A Colonel ranks just below a Brigadier General. If this had ever happened before, it had to be a rare occurrence.

January 29, 1946

I seem to remember my father saying that he got to the base a few minutes late. His orders were to put the same, or perhaps a different, B25 through the preflight checks prior to a test flight. He didn't check the roster to see who he was flying with. Dad is aboard doing his job when Smith and his copilot, also a Colonel, board the plane. This flight was only the second time Smith had piloted a B25 and it was the first time for the copilot.

Before Dad was able to finish the preflight checks, these two men wound up the plane, taxied down the runway, and lifted off. The pilot and copilot were supposed to verify Dad's preflight procedures, but apparently, they did not. My father, in the back of the plane, makes his way forward to the cockpit. When Smith sees him he says, "Well, here's the guy who won't fly with me. Looks like you're flying with me now." My Dad says, "Looks like I'm crashing with you", and crash they did.

There were air intakes that Dad didn't have a chance to be sure were open. The plane wasn't breathing and was barreling through the air a mile out, but losing altitude. The pilot tried to turn the plane around and set back down on the runway, but they didn't make it. They crashed belly down in a farmer's field, ran through barbed wire fences, and stopped abruptly in a lake. On impact, my Father was thrown from the plane into the water, sustaining a compound fracture of his leg.

As the story goes, with his leg broken and bleeding, he crawled back into the plane. The pilot and copilot were knocked out. He beat a hatch open, pulled these men from the plane, and got them to the waters edge just as help arrived.

There was a full field hospital on the base, but instead they took Dad in an ambulance to an aid station at Tinker Airfield, about 17 miles away. It's seems they wanted to removed him completely from the scene.

They couldn't give him sulfa drugs because he had been overdosed on them during a previous surgery. Why they didn't give him penicillin, only God knows, because after the war ended it was being produced and in fairly general use for both the military personnel and civilians. So, they just put his leg in a cast and as a result, his leg developed osteomyelitis which is an inflammation of bone tissue caused by infection.

At some point, Dad decided that the Air Corps couldn't or wouldn't provide proper care. He then went to the Mayo Clinic. They said that they could have done more if he had come to them sooner, but now the only option was to amputate his leg.

Over the remaining 19 years of his life he had several operations, removing more and more of his leg. I seem to recall that he told me he had spent about 3 ½ years in hospitals after the plane crash. I was also told by my mother that the last five years of his life were pretty much downhill.

My Father was a smoker. I do remember that he tried several times to stop smoking, but I don't believe he ever did really quit. Dad didn't die from smoking, but it surely was a factor.

I can narrow down the last poignant conversation with my Father to a little less than 60 days. It falls between my 12th birthday and the day he died. I walk into the family room and Dad is sitting in his chair watching TV. I say hi and he says, "Richard, come over here." He sits me down on his only knee. "Richard, how old are you?"

"I'm 12 Dad". I had just had a birthday, but at age 12, I was aware that adults often forgot things.

He said, "Well you're getting pretty big. Do you think you're too big to hug and kiss your old Dad?"

"No Dad". I was shocked. It had never occurred to me that I would have ever grown too big or become too old. This was the last time I remember hugging and kissing my father.

Very soon after that evening, my father drove himself from southwest Missouri to the Veterans Administration Hospital in Kansas City for what we thought was just another trip to the hospital. He died there on July 7, 1965, about a month before his 53RD birthday and his 25th wedding anniversary.

51 years later my brother managed to obtain the declassified official report of the crash. His name was listed as the flight engineer, but they didn't even take his statement for the report.

I loved my father.

MOM

My Mother was born Ruth Nadine Miller on June 16, 1920, on the family farm in Monroe county near the town of Mexico, Missouri. Only 30 miles away from Mexico, also in Monroe county, Mark Twain was born Samuel Langhorne Clemens in Florida, Missouri on November 30, 1835.

Somewhere in our family photographs is a picture of me when I was a child, standing in front of the log cabin where Mr. Twain was born.

Here are four quotes from Mark Twain

1. "Giving up smoking is the easiest thing in the world. I know because I've done it thousands of times. "

2. A habit cannot be tossed out the window; it must be coaxed down the stairs a step at a time."

3. "There will never be a 'perfect' time to quit smoking. A time when you don't have any distractions or stress..."

4. "The secret of getting ahead is getting started."

I didn't know these quotes when I quit smoking over 30 years ago, nor did I know them when I started writing this book. Put all four together, and you have place to start on your journey to becoming a nonsmoker.

When my father died in 1965, my mother was working for a company named Rocketdyne and commuting to Neosho, Mo. Monday through Friday. Rocketdyne built the booster engines for the Mercury space project, so while we were watching Americans go to space, we knew that Mom had done her part to help make it happen. Three years later, in 1968, my sister and brother were in college and Mom and I moved to Tulsa, Oklahoma. Rocketdyne had fallen on hard times because their contracts ran out and they didn't get contracts for the upcoming Gemini space project. Rocketdyne merged with North American Rockwell, so Mom had a job to go to in Tulsa.

In 1971 I graduated from high school and left Tulsa to start my first year in college. My Mother left her job, having earned a 10 year retirement and moved on to Oklahoma City where my brother was attending college.

She then went to work for the Veterans Administration hospital as the secretary for the chief of nuclear medicine. She had hopes of getting in a position to better pursue our claim that Dad died from an Army Air Corp service connected death. The claim wasn't recognized by the government, and our family was never compensated.

My mother never did quit cigarettes. After nearly 50 years of smoking, they quit her. Toward the end, she would light them up and watch them burn up in the ashtray. When she reached a point where she couldn't even get them burning, that's where she and her cigarettes parted company. I was a witness to that moment.

I need to say it. Emphysema is an ugly way to die, and a heartbreaking way to watch a loved one pass on. We took care of her around the clock the last year of her life.

Mom died January 23, 1989, age 68.

At that time, I was a video store manager. Around the dinner hour, I was usually the only one in the store. Although it was January, the evening was cool but not cold. I walked outside and it was dark on the ground, but the clouds to the south were still lit up by the setting sun.

As I looked up at these beautiful clouds a "knowing" came to me. I knew my mother was going to pass that night. I went inside and a few minutes later the store phone started ringing. It was my brother's wife telling me to get to the hospital as quickly as possible. By the time I got there, she was gone.

My sister Karen, the oldest sibling, was with her when she died. She had been in a coma for a few days. I was relieved that her suffering was over, and so happy that the last words we said to each other were, "I love you".

Four months later, on May 11th it was my birthday and once again I was alone in the store. I was walking around, just waiting for the next rush of customers. Then, I saw a penny on the floor. I picked it up and was delighted that it was a wheat penny, which I collect. I dropped it in my pocket and the "knowing" happened again. I knew that it was a 1953 penny, the year of my birth. I took it out of my pocket and, yes it was a 1953! I choose to believe my mother was wishing me happy birthday!

Not long before her death, she asked how long it had been since I was a smoker. The answer I gave was something over 2 ½ years. She said, "Rick, I think you have really quit". I said, "You know Mom, I think I really have."

She settled back in her bed with a smile on her face. She passed on knowing that I wasn't going to die from smoking. I loved my Mother.

THE FUTURE

I've never been one for long range planning. However, I have made decisions that had a positive effect on my future. My quitting smoking is the prime example.

"Every saint has a past and every sinner has a future."
–Oscar Wilde

...and what will your future bring? We can move forward with no plan at all and let the future wash over us, come what may. Or...we can make plans, set goals, and work toward what we truly want and what we would love to see happen in our lives.

There are worse things than tobacco to be addicted to, but not many, and not by much. You should quit smoking as if your life depends on it, because it truly might. No matter who you are, you deserve better. The goodness and abundance of life can and should be yours. Quitting tobacco is a wise investment in the future that awaits you.

DON'T LET YOUR FUTURE GO UP IN SMOKE !

JOURNAL

Made in the USA
Middletown, DE
20 October 2022